D0754713

Haunted Houses Real?

BY PATRICK PERISH

amicus
high interest

Amicus High Interest is published by Amicus
P.O. Box 1329, Mankato, MN 56002
www.amicuspublishing.us

Library of Congress Cataloging-in-Publication Data
Perish, Patrick.
 Are haunted houses real? / by Patrick Perish.
    pages cm. -- (Unexplained: what's the evidence?)
 Includes bibliographical references and index.
 Summary: "Presents famous haunted houses such as the
Borley Rectory, the White House, and the Amityville horror,
and briefly examines the claims, some of which have no
scientific explanation and some of which were hoaxes"--
Provided by publisher.
 ISBN 978-1-60753-385-6 (library binding) --
ISBN 978-1-60753-433-4 (ebook)
 1. Haunted houses--Juvenile literature. I. Title.
 BF1475.P47 2014
 133.1'22--dc23

                         2012047566

Editor   Rebecca Glaser
Series Designer   Kathleen Petelinsek
Page production   Red Line Editorial, Inc.

Photo Credits
Shutterstock Images, cover; Jim Leach/123RF, 5; Library
of Congress, 6, 19, 20; Henry Justice Ford, 9; Ewan
Chesser/123RF, 11; William Attard McCarthy/123RF, 12;
Public Domain, 15; Dan Risso/123RF, 16; Paul Hawthorne/
Getty Images, 23; Ted Rhodes/Windsor Star/AP Images,
24; Jim Hannon/Times Daily/AP Images, 27; Thye Aun
Ngo/123RF, 28

Printed in the United States of America at Corporate Graphics
in North Mankato, Minnesota.
1/2014 / P.O. 1194
10 9 8 7 6 5 4 3

Table of Contents

Are Houses Haunted?   4

First Reports   8

Famous Haunted Houses   14

Exposing the Fakes   22

What's the Evidence?   26

Glossary   30

Read More   31

Websites   31

Index   32

Are Houses Haunted?

Can a house really be haunted? An old house covered in cobwebs seems creepy. At Halloween, maybe you've walked through a "haunted house." It's not really haunted, though. But some say there are houses with real ghosts.

Old, empty houses can seem spooky.

4

People have seen ghosts in the Whaley House in California.

Several types of ghosts are said to haunt houses. Some are people who died in the house. Their ghosts stay. The Whaley family lived in San Diego, California. Now their ghosts appear in their old house. Some ghosts are **invisible**. They break things and make messes. Some ghosts do the same things over and over, like a recording.

First Reports

Stories of haunted houses have been around for ages. This story is from ancient Greece. In Athens, a brave man bought an old, haunted house. The ghost in the house had chains on his wrists. He wanted the man to follow him outside. Then it disappeared! The man marked the spot. He dug and found bones and chains! He buried them in a graveyard. The ghost never came back.

A ghost with chains haunted a man in an ancient Greek story.

Many old **castles** are said to be haunted. Castle Grant is in Scotland. The music of a ghostly piper has been heard in the castle walls. In the kitchen, ghost maids have been seen. They wash invisible plates. A chief's daughter was locked in the tower once. At night her ghost wanders the halls.

Scotland has many old castles.
This one is Castle Fraser.

People say they have seen
ghosts both inside and outside.

Q What is the Society for Psychical Research?

In 1882, a student in England named Rosina Despard saw a ghost in her house. It was a tall lady. It went downstairs and out to the yard. Then it disappeared! Rosina was not scared. She took notes. She sent them to the Society for Psychical Research. The ghost came many times. At least 17 people saw it.

 It is a group of scientists in London. They look into things that science can't explain. They share what they learn with other scientists.

Famous Haunted Houses

The Borley **Rectory** was a house in England. In 1863, a family moved in. They heard footsteps and taps on the walls. They saw a headless man in the garden. Strange writing appeared on the wall. Harry Price, the ghost hunter, checked it out. He said it was the most haunted house in England. It burned down in 1939.

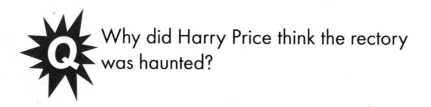 Why did Harry Price think the rectory was haunted?

The Borley Rectory was said to be haunted until it burned down.

A His team saw strange things. A candlestick flew down the stairs. A brick crashed through a window. They couldn't explain it.

The Winchester Mystery House is in San Jose, California.

Q Can anyone go inside the Winchester mansion?

In 1884, Sarah Winchester started to build a **mansion**. Legends say it was full of angry spirits. Workers built it for 38 years. It was seven stories tall when they were done. The rooms twist around. Some doors open on blank walls. Some staircases have hundreds of tiny steps. Some say Sarah built it to hide from spirits.

 Yes. People can visit and take a tour. Some people report seeing ghosts there.

The Fairbanks House is in Massachusetts. It was built around 360 years ago. Weird things happen there. Flashlights go dead. The security alarm goes off for no reason. The caretaker called a ghost-hunting team. The ghost hunters heard footsteps when no one was there. They recorded strange knocks and whispers. They could not explain the sounds.

Strange things seem to happen in the Fairbanks House.

The ghost of Abe Lincoln has appeared in the Lincoln Room.

Q Who has seen Lincoln's ghost?

Even the White House could be haunted. Visitors have spotted the ghost of Abe Lincoln inside. Sometimes he stares out a window. Other times he takes off his boots. He is seen near the Lincoln Room the most. Abigail Adams was the wife of the second president, John Adams. Her ghost has been seen near the East Room.

 Grace, the wife of President Coolidge, was the first to see it. Queen Wilhelmina of the Netherlands and Winston Churchill also saw it.

Exposing the Fakes

Many haunted houses are fake. The most famous was in Amityville, New York. In 1974, a family was murdered. The Lutzes bought their house. They said doors were flung open. Slime oozed from the walls. A **demon** even left tracks in the snow! Their story was made into movies. Later, **investigators** checked it out. The whole thing was made up.

 How did they know the story was made up?

This house in Amityville is a
famous, but fake, haunted house.

After the Lutzes moved out, other people
moved in. They did not see ghosts. The Lutz's
lawyer later admitted that the story was fake.

A teen in Canada made news
when he faked a ghost.

24

In 1997, a ghost named Sommy haunted a family in Canada. They heard the ghost over the phone. It burped and spoke gibberish. The power turned off and on by itself. The TV channels changed on their own. News teams investigated but found nothing. Finally, the son said he was the ghost. He only started it as a joke.

What's the Evidence?

Ghost hunters try to find proof for haunted houses. They record spooky sounds. They film strange things. They use **meters** to measure energy in a room. But these haven't been proven to work. Scientists say better tests need to be done.

Ghost hunters study houses where strange things have happened.

Our minds might trick us into thinking an old house is haunted.

 Q How many people believe in haunted houses?

Haunted houses are a mystery. Some say the dead hang around. They get attached to places. Others say haunted houses are only tricks of the mind. Creaky old houses only look creepy. People imagine the ghosts. There isn't enough proof yet to say who's right. Maybe in time the mystery can be unlocked.

 A poll was taken in 2005. More than one-third of Americans who answered believe in haunted houses!

Glossary

castle A large stone building often surrounded by a wall and a moat.

demon An evil spirit.

investigator Someone who tries to find out all the facts of a story to figure out what really happened.

invisible Unable to be seen.

mansion A very large and grand house with many rooms.

meter A machine that measures something.

rectory A home for a pastor and his or her family.

Read More

Chandler, Matt. *The World's Most Haunted Places.* Mankato, Minn.: Capstone Press, 2012.

Parvis, Sarah E. *Haunted Hotels.* New York: Bearport Pub., 2008.

Perish, Patrick. *Are Ghosts Real?* Mankato, Minn.: Amicus, 2014.

Williams, Dinah. *Haunted Houses.* New York: Bearport Pub., 2008.

Websites

FamilyCorner.com — Create Your Own Haunted House
http://www.familycorner.com/family/kids/halloween/ haunted_house.shtml

Ghostvillage — Paranormal investigating
http://kids.ghostvillage.com/

The World's Most Haunted Castles
http://kids.aol.com/2012/06/04/the-worlds-most- haunted-castles/

Index

Adams, Abigail 21

Amityville, New York 22–23

Borley Rectory 14–15

Castle Grant 10

Despard, Rosina 13

England 13, 14

Fairbanks House 18, 19

ghost hunters 14, 18, 26

Greece 8

Halloween 4

Lincoln, Abe 20–21

Price, Harry 14–15

Sommy 25

Society for Psychical Research 12–13

spirits 17

Whaley House 6, 7

White House 21

Winchester Mystery House 16–17

Winchester, Sarah 17

About the Author

Patrick Perish spent many childhood nights under the covers with a flashlight and good book. In particular, aliens, ghosts, and other unexplained mysteries have always kept him up until the wee hours of the night. He lives in Minneapolis, MN where he writes and edits children's books.